Mr. McTavish Goes to the Library

Bon Kay

Fulton Books, Inc.
Meadville, PA

Published by Fulton Books 2021

ISBN 978-1-64952-119-4 (paperback)
ISBN 978-1-63710-821-5 (hardcover)
ISBN 978-1-64952-120-0 (digital)

Printed in the United States of America

Gma said one of the magic words—*ride*. I love rides. I am hopping up and down with happiness. Gma takes me on wonderful fun rides. I wonder where we are going today. Oh, here she comes with my leash. Yippee!

Jumping into the front seat of her car is exciting for a Scotty with stubby legs. But I'm strong and can make it easily all the way up into my riding box. Gma is always sure to buckle me up before we leave. My special box helps me look out all the front and side windows.

I can see cars coming toward us and people walking along on the sidewalks. There are always these three lights, sometimes green or yellow or red. Gma seems to know what they mean. I am glad of that! There are lots of noisy cars like ours moving around outside. I would not want to bump into one of them.

Today it seems to take a little longer to get to where we are going. But soon the car slows up, and she pulls into a parking space. She reaches down into my bag and pulls out my hat. I didn't like my hat at first, but it has grown on me. I have gotten lots of "Oh, how cute!" and "Doesn't he look dashing?" remarks when I wear it. We only go to special places when I wear my hat, so this must be a special place.

There is this big long building in front of us, and there seems to be many big and little people outside, waving at us. Gma comes around to my door and helps me out of my buckle up and secures my leash. As I jumped down from my box, Gma is saying something to a woman who has walked forward to greet us.

The woman looks down at me and says, "Hello, Mr. McTavish. We are so glad you have come today." And my ears perk up.

I knew my name and saw a big smile on her face. I feel there is going to be lots of fun here today. She bends down and gives me a light tickle behind my ear. I have a new friend.

After more handshaking and talk, Gma says come, and we head up the walkway beside this woman toward all the other people who are giggling and waving and jumping up and down just like I do. I start to prance with joy and know this is going to be a great adventure.

ABC ELEMENTARY

MAIN ENTRANCE

SERVICE

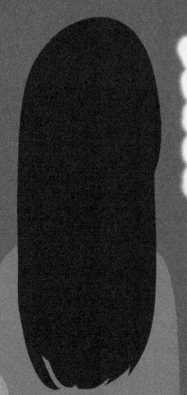

Everyone parts as we enter the building, and we are walking down a long hallway. We come to a big door with windows in it, and I can see more people inside. The door opens, and Gma and I walk into cheers and clapping. I have never had anyone cheer me before. I like it!

Gma and I are taken over to rows of chairs that are lined up between all these shelves of books. I have never seen so many books. Gma has some that she sits and reads all the time, but not this many. Gma sits down in the middle of the front row, and I sit beside her feet.

The woman that greeted us is now standing behind this high square table and starts to talk into a black tube coming from it. She is looking at us and gesturing while she is talking.

"Everyone, I want to introduce you to Ms. Beatrice and her buddy Mr. McTavish. They are here today, so we can thank them in person for their generous gift to our library. They made the donation so we could purchase our iPad charger cart that streamlines our ability to charge all our iPads overnight. We are so very grateful to them."

Applause and cheers fill the whole area. Gma looks so happy.

From the side of the room, someone is rolling out this large cart with all these square black boxes lined up on it. These must be the iPads they are talking about. The kids are now jumping up and down again and pointing to the cart. Gma is clapping now and laughing with everyone.

Gma gets up and tells me to come. We walk up to the box, and she turns around to face everyone. I stand at a heel by her side, and I am feeling very proud.

Gma says, "I want to thank you all for this wonderful welcome that you have given me and Mr. McTavish. We are overjoyed that our small gift has given everyone here such joy and happiness. I'm sure it will continue to make many students in the future as happy as you are now. That is a wonderful feeling to have that we could make many students happy for many years to come."

Many cheers and claps later, we are given treats and drinks, and soon we are on our way home after many thank-yous from everyone.

I'm sitting by Gma's side, and I'm very proud and happy too. This has been a wonderful day for a ride.

I wonder if we will have more wonderful days like this one?

About the Author

Bon Kay has lived in Pennsylvania all her life and a Central, Pennsylvania resident for over forty-two years. Becoming an author in her retirement, she was inspired to start a series of stories based on her Scotty dog, McTavish, who was her buddy for almost twelve years. Tavi, as he was nicknamed, rarely barked and loved everyone, especially those who tickled behind his ear. She hopes her Mr. McTavish series will inspire others.

9 781649 521194